5 SIMPLE WAYS

TO ♥ SAY

"I LOVE YOU"

Stephen Arterburn
& Carl Dreizler

OLIVER
NELSON

A Division of Thomas Nelson Publishers
Nashville

Published in Nashville, Tennessee, by Oliver-Nelson Books, a division of Thomas Nelson, Inc., Publishers, and distributed in Canada by Lawson Falle, Ltd., Cambridge, Ontario.

Printed in the United States of America.

Library of Congress Cataloging-in-Publication Data

Arterburn, Stephen, 1953–
    52 simple ways to say I love you / Stephen Arterburn & Carl Dreizler.
       p.   cm.
    ISBN 0-8407-9523-8
    1. Interpersonal relations—Miscellanea.   2. Love—Miscellanea.
I. Dreizler, Carl, 1954–   . II. Title.   III. Title: Fifty-two
simple ways to say I love you.
HM132.A75   1991
158.2—dc20   90-48579
                                              CIP

2 3 4 5 6 — 96 95 94 93 92 91

❤ Contents

❤ Introduction

Throughout the pages of this book are fifty-two simple ways to tell the important people in your life how much you love them. Some of the ideas are new. Some of them are as old as mankind itself. Our hope is that you will pick up this book and use it to say "I love you" in many different ways.

Just saying "I love you" is not enough, for loving someone is not merely saying the right words. The best way we can say "I love you" is to spend increasing amounts of time with the people we love. Most of the fifty-two ideas presented here provide you with ways to say you love someone and to confirm that love through time together.

We've purposely written each idea so that almost all of them could be used by any two people who love one another. Husbands and wives. Mothers and daughters. Fathers and sons. Lifelong friends. Use these ideas with your grandparents. Grandchildren. Family. Friends.

If your goal, however, is to create more sparks in your romance with someone, each of these ideas can lead to that end. This book will teach you to have lots of fun in any loving relationship. We hope it will also help you gain the respect of people close to you. And because they will see you as a fun and loving person, you will probably feel lots better about yourself.

Look through the ideas. If you've always found it hard to say "I love you," start with one idea that doesn't seem too threatening. Try it out. Then move on to another idea. Before long, you may find yourself thinking of your own new ways to say "I love you."

There are fifty-two ideas in this book, enough for one a week for a year. You should never run out of ways to express your love for someone. You can use some of these ideas time and time again. And you can add your own personal touches to the suggestions included.

We hope this book will be a useful tool for building a stronger bond with the important people in your life. From the lonely neighbor next door or the son you never seem to find time for to your relationship with the person you love most, we are convinced you can grow stronger together.

1 ♥ Moonlight Walk

How wonderful to walk a mile
In the morning or at noon
But he or she will like your style
If that walk's beneath the moon

The Idea: Talk about a simple idea! Yet how often have you purposely taken a walk under a full moon? This idea is especially appropriate for those who are in a relationship where romance is a factor. If you want to woo your sweetie, this one's for you.

Yet, this idea is appropriate for any two people who love each other. Even for those nonromantic relationships with loved ones, there's still something magical about a walk in the moonlight, something that makes the heart more tender and willing to express feelings.

Planning Your Walk: This event needs little planning. In fact, it can be done on the spur of the moment. Look outside tonight. If the moon is full, drop everything, grab the one you love, and find a quiet, open spot away from the crowd.

If you want to plan your moonlight stroll, find out when the next full moon will be. Go a step further, and find out what time the moon is rising and setting. You can find this information by checking your local newspaper or by calling either your local weather bureau or public library.

Selecting Your Setting: While you always have the option of walking beneath the moonlight near your home, the best moonlight walks take place where there are wide-open spaces. You're lucky if you live near a desert. In the mountains, search for a place that overlooks the lower elevations. In the winter, seek a place where the moon will reflect off newly fallen snow.

If you live near a large body of water, time your walk so you can see the moon rise or set above it. There's something beautiful about moonlight shining on a body of water.

What to Say: We don't need to tell you what to say. That will take care of itself. There's something about a full moon. . . .

2 ❤ The Retreat

Pack a lunch and get away
Your life should not be dull
Leave the dishes one more day
The office in-box full

The Idea: Because our weekends or other days off become as hectic and filled with chores as the days we work or go to school, we must plan special days with friends and loved ones. Why not say "I love you" by setting aside one full day to go away with the one you love for a time of reflection and introspection?

This event should not take place as part of a company picnic or during a day you were planning at the beach or park for some other occasion. This day should be scheduled solely for the purpose described below. This retreat is recommended for two people rather than groups or entire families.

Preparing for the Big Day:

1. Pick a place that is special to the two of you. While it is difficult in many parts of the world to find totally isolated spots, try to make this your primary goal. Perhaps you know of a hiking trail in the mountains, an isolated beach, a cabin in the wilderness, or a stream in the woods.

2. Set the date with the one you love.

3. Review the "Reflections" sample included in this section. Feel free to alter the sample and produce your own final copy. Make two copies of your Reflections sheet. Write your name in the blank space at the top of the sheet you will be giving to the one you love. Write the other person's name in the blank for the Reflections sheet you will keep. Put these and two or three pens in an envelope. Don't forget to take the envelope with you!

A Suggested Schedule for Your Day:

8:00 a.m.   Pack a picnic lunch with your favorite snacks and beverages. It might be fun to splurge on this one and use the picnic basket rather than brown paper bags. But since this is a day of rest and relaxation, use whatever you want.

9:00 a.m.   Say goodbye to everyone else who isn't going and head out the door.

10:30 a.m.   Arrive at your special place. Take a walk, talk, and just enjoy being together. But don't get into topics to be discussed later. Maybe you'll want to hold hands (if appropriate). This is the warming-up period, a time to enjoy the serenity of your new environment.

If you or your partner have a hard time leaving work and worries behind, here are two ideas that might help:

- *Pick up a rock. While holding it in your hands, speak to the rock, saying, "I am placing all the stress of my job, my finances, my relationships and everything else into you today. This is my day to relax. Hope you enjoy your day holding all these burdens for me just as I will enjoy mine without them." Toss the rock far from you, thereby releasing all your worries—at least for this day.*

- *Breathe deeply. Move your head in slow, easy circles about your neck. Shake your left arm as a way to represent one thing on your mind that you want to clear out for the day. Do the same thing with your right arm to release another distraction. If you've got more, shake both of your legs.*

12:00 p.m.   Find a relaxing spot and eat lunch. After lunch lie down on your backs and look straight up into the sky or at the branches above you if you happen to be under a tree. Talk about what you see. Talk about your thoughts.

1:30 p.m.   Explain to the one you love that you each will go to separate places for the next two hours. Pick an easy spot to find for your reunion at about 3:30. Tell your companion to think about your relationship since its inception as you both walk to your separate private places. Before parting, give the other person the appropriate Reflections sheet and a pen. Ask him or her to complete each thought with a sentence or paragraph before you rejoin. You do the same.

3:30 p.m.   Meet at your agreed-upon spot. Share with one another what you have written. Look him or her in the eyes as you read. Try to be tender.
You may want to alternate reading your responses to the Reflec-

tions items or have one person at a time read the entire sheet.

5:30 p.m.   Walk together for a half hour reflecting silently on what just happened. Try not to talk during this last part of your day.

6:00 p.m.   Hug the one you love and tell that person you love him or her. Your special retreat is over.

Reflections

Complete each thought with a few sentences expressing your deepest feelings about _____ .

The first time I met you . . .

I first knew I loved you when . . .

My favorite memory with you is . . .

My favorite thing about you is . . .

The thing I've always wanted to tell you but never have is . . .

My favorite part of this day with you has been . . .

The promise I make to you today with regard to our future is . . .

3 ♥ Are You Interested?

Find the interest they like most
Something you have never done
Take the hobby that they boast
You just might have some fun!

The Idea: I'm sure your loved one has a hobby, interest, or pastime that you have always thought was a waste of time or was something you would never want to do. Well, it's time you mount that dirt bike or search for that red bird with the yellow bill, if only for a day or two.

In every relationship both parties should have activities they like to do on their own. It's healthy to have separate and individual interests. But showing an interest in someone else's favorite pastime, if only in a limited way, is an expression of love. So begin now to plan a day for the two of you (or for the family) to do that special hobby together.

Preparing for the Big Day: The first thing you need to do is sit down and think about all the hobbies and interests of the one you love. List five of them here:

_____

_____

_____

_____

_____

Now rank them by putting a 1 in front of the hobby he or she would be most shocked to see you take part in, and a 5 before the item he or she would find the least shocking. Now, you decide which activity you will participate in. Will you pick the one you can most tolerate, or the one the other person would never, in a million years, expect you to do?

Announcing Your Interest: You have at least two options here.

> 1. Tell the one you love to reserve a day for something special, and make it a surprise when you tell him that morning you will be joining him for a day of deep-sea fishing.

> 2. If you want to make the shock less dramatic, you can tell the person what you have in mind when you set up the date initially. This may be the courteous thing to do if you want to make sure you have picked her favorite beach for skin diving.

Compounding Your Interest: You may choose to make this a low-key event or go all out. Here are some ways to make the day even more memorable:

- Buy or borrow the outfit that is typical for this hobby, and greet your friend all decked out in your special clothes. If you are going bird watching, buy the red and black flannel shirt, special pants, and inventory book. Oh, and be sure to have your binoculars around your neck.

- If you really want to make the day special, invite all his buddies or her girlfriends to go, saying that you just want to be one of the gang.

- Read up on the hobby or interest so you will sound as though you know what you are talking about.

Above all, enjoy yourself!

4 ♥ Hour Class

Today before they go away
Put a note inside the shower
But don't just give them one today
Write them one for every hour

The Idea: Imagine receiving not just one message of love from someone, but a message an hour for one full day. Here's the idea. One selected morning, give the one you love a stack of envelopes. On the front of each one will be the time of day, one envelope for each hour from 7:00 a.m. to 10:00 p.m. That's sixteen envelopes in all.

Inside each envelope will be special messages of love written by you. The person you love will open one each hour as marked. This idea may be one of the simplest and yet most memorable ones of the fifty-two in this book. Try it.

Selecting the Right Day: This idea is best suited for a working day or some other time when you will not be with the one you love. The notes may have more meaning when you are not around. And the one you love may be more anxious than ever before to see you at the end of the day.

Going the Extra Mile: For a little added fun, slip some small gift into a few or into all of the envelopes. Use photos of the two of you or of others in your life whom you both love. Hand write a certificate good for a romantic dinner with you. Insert a piece of chewing gum. Include a picture drawn by one of your children. Put lipstick on your lips and then kiss a piece of paper.

Preparing Your Messages:

You can implement this idea on any budget. You can write your notes on lined paper and use business envelopes or go all out and buy sixteen different greeting cards. You can also use personal stationery to make each note look the same or use a variety of things to make each package as different from one another as possible.

Plan your notes wisely, perhaps saving the most sentimental and deeply felt messages for the hours closest to your getting together that evening. Here are some ideas for various times throughout the day. These are notes from Bob written to his wife, Ann.

7:00 a.m.
(Placed in the shower or near the bathroom sink)

Ann, by the time this day is over, I want one thing to be perfectly clear in your mind—the fact that I love you. After you take your shower and get ready for work, pick up the stack of envelopes I put near your briefcase. Open each one only at the time marked on the outside of the envelope. I'll be thinking about you as you open them. Have a fun day.

12:00 p.m.

By now you should be having lunch. I wish I could be there to eat with you. Remember the day we had the picnic down at Little Falls? That was the first day I knew I really loved you. I still do. I've enclosed a piece of gum as a treat for you when you finish eating. Enjoy it.

5:00 p.m.

If you're like me right now, you probably thought this day would never end. Come on home. I'll have dinner waiting for you. It's your favorite. I've enclosed a cartoon I saw in the Sunday paper. Maybe it will give you something to smile about as you drive home.

10:00 p.m.

This may be the last note of this special day, but it certainly will not be the last time I tell you how much I love you. Come and see me right now. I'll tell you in person this time. Good night. You're a very special woman.

5 ❤ Love Defined

Love is patient; Love is kind
Though no two define it the same
Take this example and see what you find
Replace the word "love" with your name

The Idea: What better way to show your love for another person than by evaluating your own ability to display love. What a difficult word *love* is to define. Perhaps the best description of love is found in the New Testament book of First Corinthians:

> *Love is patient*
> *Love is kind*
> *It is not jealous*
> *Love does not brag*
> *And it is not arrogant*
>
> *Love does not act unbecomingly*
> *It does not seek its own way*
> *It is not provoked*
> *Love does not take into account a wrong suffered*
> *It does not rejoice in unrighteousness*
> *But rejoices in truth*
>
> *Love bears all things*
> *Believes all things*
> *Hopes all things*
> *Endures all things*
>
> *Love never fails**

* 1 Corinthians 13:4–8, paraphrased from the New American Standard Bible.

Assessing Yourself as One Who Is Loving:

One genuine way to say "I love you" is to work on becoming a person who is more loving with each day. Try the following exercise as regularly as you can, *especially* when life gets tough and you don't feel as though you are as loving as you could be.

Take the above definition of love, and insert your name everywhere the word *love* or its pronoun appears. Let's use someone named Ken as an example:

> *Ken is patient*
> *Ken is kind*
> *Ken is not jealous*
> *Ken does not brag*
> *And Ken is not arrogant*
>
> *Ken does not act unbecomingly*
> *Ken does not seek his own way*
> *Ken is not provoked*
> *Ken does not take into account a wrong suffered*
> *Ken does not rejoice in unrighteousness*
> *But rejoices in truth*
>
> *Ken bears all things*
> *Believes all things*
> *Hopes all things*
> *Endures all things*
>
> *Ken never fails*

Is it possible to pass all of these tests? Of course not. Especially the last one. We all fail in one way or another every day. But the goal is to use this model to analyze how well you love. Use it often. Then work on the areas where you fall short.

Any improvement you make in yourself tells the ones you love how much you care about them.

6 ❤ Sunrise, Sunset

You find yourself all over town
Your days, they just go by
But stand and watch the sun go down
You'll stop and wonder why

The Idea: Whenever we take time out of a busy schedule to sit in a favorite spot and watch the sun complete its day, we often wonder why we work so hard, why other things take precedence over this simple experience. Most of us could watch the sunset every night for the rest of our lives and never get bored.

If your favorite place to watch a sunset happens to be a place where other people go to view the same phenomenon, observe them next time you go. Just before sunset, people will stop walking, stop talking, and simply gaze at the sign from God that another day has ended.

Make watching the sunset a common event with the one you love. Each day as you watch the sun go down, say, "I love you." We never really know if we will be there when the sun sets tomorrow.

Reviewing Your Day: Every day that you watch the sunset with people you love, take a few moments to find out how their day went. We often don't take time to ask such simple questions as, "How was your day?" Nor do we take the time to listen to the responses. Here are some other suggestions for your conversations with loved ones at the end of a busy day.

- Thank each one for something he or she did for you today.
- Ask what you can do to be more supportive.
- Tell a special someone you are glad to be sharing the sunset with him or her.
- Share something for which you are grateful to God.
- Ask what their favorite part of the day was.
- Encourage them in any trials they may be facing.
- Tell them how much they mean to you.
- Say, "I love you."
- Invite them to watch the sunset with you tomorrow night, too.

An Alternative: If you and the one you love are both early risers, or if evening schedules prevent sunset viewings, try finding a special place to watch the sunrise. Instead of reviewing the day and seeing it come to a close, reflect on the promises each new day provides. Spend part of your time listening to the new day beginning. Start the new day by saying, "I love you." Few things can ruin any day that begins with these three words.

7 ♥ Carin' Valentine

Guess it all comes down to this
The day that's made for love
For first romance or marital bliss
Just thank our God above

The Idea: For Valentine's Day, you probably have a lot of your own ideas. But here are some suggestions to make the day that was made for love even more special.

Making the Next Valentine's Day the Best Ever:

- *Make the largest Valentine card* you can imagine. Find a refrigerator carton, paint a heart and Valentine message on it, and then stand it up in your living room on Valentine's Day.

- *Put a message in front of your house* using a real estate sign with cardboard taped over the realtor's information. Instead write "Inside this house is the most wonderful wife in the world. Her name is _____."

- *Instead of buying candy this year,* make the candy yourself, and then give it to the one you love. Don't worry if it looks home-made. The effort you took will mean more than the candy's appearance.

- *In addition to sending roses* or instead of sending roses, bring them home with you. If you live in a place where flowers grow year-round, go together to a place where you can walk and pick your own bouquet.

- *Buy Valentine's Day cards,* not just for the most significant person in your life, but for other people who may never receive Valentines.

8 ♥ Plan a Treasure Hunt

Check the tape deck, push rewind
Do what you are told
You're the treasure they will find
Who needs silver or gold?

The Idea: This idea is lots of fun. You will be a pirate who has buried a treasure and has recorded its whereabouts in code. The one you love is the lucky explorer who finds the clues leading to the secret treasure—and the secret treasure is you!

It might be fun for two or three couples to implement this idea together. The husbands can be the pirates, the wives the explorers. Or you may want to have your whole family participate, or perhaps a group of friends.

Planning Your Treasure Hunt: First, set a date with the one you love, explaining that he must leave your house, or not arrive there, until a specified time that you designate. Tell him he must be prompt, but not early. Your loved one will be thinking you have planned a wonderful surprise party and will expect people to jump out and hug him when he enters the house. Instead, he will find an empty house and the first of many clues leading to the "buried treasure."

Much to your friend's surprise, he will not find an old treasure chest filled to the limit with jewels, gold, and silver. Instead, you will be seated at a favorite restaurant, waiting with a fresh bouquet of flowers or tickets to a play you both have been wanting to see. How romantic.

The Treasure Hunt: Here's where you can use your imagination. Carefully plan a series of ten to twelve clues, each of which leads to the next and the last of which leads to you! But you're going to need an escape hatch—just in case your clues are too clever. You don't want to be stranded in some romantic restaurant, sitting alone with wilted flowers.

To solve this dilemma, and to help you get started, we've provided a suggestion for your first note, which must be placed where the other person is sure to find it. Be sure he has a way to get into the house. Remember, he's expecting you to be there.

CLUES TO THE SECRET TREASURE

Congratulations! You have just found the first clue that, if followed correctly, will lead you to a secret treasure. Begin your treasure hunt as soon as you read this note, or you will miss out on a great opportunity!

But First, A Word of Caution

If this puzzle gets too tough,
   no treasure have you found.
At eight o'clock be by the phone,
   'cause I want you around.
I'll tell you where the treasure is,
   and where you have to go.
But try to solve this simple game;
   the first clue is below.

CLUE 1: Look into my ice.

You'll find the location of Clue 2 there.

(If you can't figure this out, look at the back of this paper. But try to solve the clues on your own.)

On the back of Clue 1 you would write, "Clue 2 is in the freezer." This is again to ensure that you don't get stranded. If you think the one you love is clever enough to figure out your clues, don't bother with the easy answers.

Proceed with all your clues until the final one tells how to get to the restaurant where you are located. It might read something like this:

CLUE 12:

There's a restaurant down the street,
the one where we like to eat.

> The address is Two Two Four Nine Three
> that is where the treasure'll be.

Again, if you think your clue will seem unclear, write the name of the restaurant on the back. Once there, the one you love can celebrate the victory of finding the "buried treasure" by spending an evening with you.

Dry Run: Before you leave the house, do a dry run to make sure you left the clues in the right order. Is this one of the more simple ideas in this book? Nah! But it's so much fun we had to put it in!

9 ❤ Put Another Candle On

The one you love is one year older
Their bones may start to creak
So this year plan events much bolder
Celebrate all week

The Idea: This year instead of celebrating only the actual birthday of the one you love, celebrate the entire preceding week!

Planning a Week-Long Birthday Celebration: Here are a few ideas to get you started.

Count down the days until his or her birthday. One week before the birthday, and on each day thereafter, start a countdown by giving the person you love a card or by placing a big sign somewhere in the house (such as on the refrigerator or on the car windshield) saying "Seven more days until your birthday!"

Ask a different friend or family member to surprise the person on each of the countdown days. Tell each person you contact that he or she is responsible for doing something special (along with you) for the one you love. The seventh day prior to the birthday may be a good time for the people at work to throw some kind of surprise lunch. The sixth day may involve your loved one's two best friends, who greet the person as he or she is leaving work for the day. And so on.

Give the person you love a gift each day. Even if you don't have a big budget, you can give gifts that have some special significance each day. You may want the gifts to relate to each other, such as different parts of a new outfit or different tapes of the person's favorite music.

Throw a surprise party. You may want to throw a surprise party on day four or five. Because you are doing all these other crazy things, the person might expect a surprise party on the exact birthday. This will catch him or her off guard.

Make the actual birthday day extra-special in some way. Because you have prepared all these different surprises throughout the week, you don't want the actual birthday to be a letdown. So end the birthday week with a nice dinner between the two of you or with the family, bestowing your final gifts and perhaps presenting a scrapbook of the week's events.

When the person you love goes to bed on that birthday night, he or she will know at least two things: you don't forget birthdays, and you love him or her very much!

10 ♥ Singin' in the Rain

*Next time your plans are
    altered
Because of sudden rain
Don't let your day be faltered
The sunshine's loss, your gain*

The Idea: Are you disappointed when a free day is spoiled by an unexpected rainstorm? Don't allow it! Remember as a child how much fun it was to go out in the rain? You would find the deepest puddles to splash in. You may have dropped a leaf in some gutter filled with rushing water and followed it down the block until it disappeared into a drain. Now you can make the best of a rainy day with the one you love.

"But we might get wet!" you say. That's the point. If you don't get wet, this idea may not be any fun at all. Put on your raincoat, your galoshes, and a hat.

Ways to Have Fun When the Weather Gets Dreary:

Plan a picnic lunch. You don't have to eat *in* the rain, but find a covered patio in a nearby park. Everyone has picnics in the sunshine. You'd be surprised how much fun it is to do things that are out of the ordinary.

Reenact your favorite movie scene in the rain.
Perhaps the most memorable rainy movie
scene was Gene Kelly's famous walk and
dance down the street while he was crooning,
"Singin' in the Rain." Or the gazebo scene
from "The Sound of Music." Find a gazebo.
You may feel you are "sixteen going on sev-
enteen" again.

Take a walk in the rain. This is the simplest
idea yet within this category. Just grab an um-
brella and take a walk arm-in-arm. It might
just bring you closer emotionally than you've
been in a while.

Regress to childhood. Take the one you love
outside in the rain and find the deepest puddles. See who can splash the most water on
the other. See who can roll down the hill the
farthest. Put on some old clothes. Abandon
your adulthood, and just get wet!

View the storm. Find a special place to view
the storm. If you are near the ocean, sit in a
restaurant overlooking the stormy sea. If it's
a thunderstorm, find a place with a view so
you can watch this amazing phenomenon. If
you are too tired for anything else, just build a
fire and gaze out the window together.

11 ♥ Home, James

Gather up your loved one's friends
Get a chauffeur's hat
Where you go it all depends
On where they want you at

The Idea: Give the one you love a day or evening with friends. You don't even have to treat them to anything. Just offer to be their chauffeur for the afternoon or evening.

Here's the plan. Just tell the one you love (wife, husband, daughter, son, or anyone else you love) that you want him or her to select two or three friends (depending on the size of your car) for an afternoon or evening of fun. The agenda is theirs, although you might suggest they plan several stops for the evening so they can take full advantage of your services. Otherwise, you may be bored, sitting in the car for hours while they attend a double feature or sit through a three-hour concert.

Things You Might Need: The following are suggestions of what you might need to make this event a success. As with other suggestions in this book, you may choose to be as simple or as extravagant as you want, depending on how much money you have and how much time you want to spend planning the event.

The car. You have quite a few options here.

The simplest solution is to use your own car, as is. Or you may want to pretend it's a limo by putting a small flag on the antennae and a sign on the back that says "limo." A middle-of-the-road option is to use a friend's Lincoln or Cadillac for the evening. If you want to go all out, there are classic car rental agencies in some cities that will rent a limo for the evening.

The Outfit. At the simple end of the scale, wear a dark suit or skirt and jacket with a white shirt and black bow tie. If you want to go all out, rent a tuxedo.

Perhaps you can find some white gloves. In any case, you've got to get one of those black hats chauffeurs wear in the movies.

The Equipment. Whether you are in your own car, a friend's car, or a rented car, you can stock up the back seat with goodies found in a limousine (as long as you follow the law, of course). Start with an ice bucket containing a chilled bottle of sparkling water or cider. Of course you must have some fine stemware glasses for serving purposes. Cheese and crackers might be a nice touch too. If you have access to one, set up a battery-operated television set. Beyond these, use your own imagination to make the ride classic and memorable.

Etiquette. Always open the doors for your passengers. Offer them your hand for getting in and out of the car. Call the ladies "ma'am" and the gentlemen "sir." At each stop, clean up the back seat, replacing used glasses with new ones. Pick up and drop off each passenger at their place of residence. Change your name to "James."

12 ♥ When You Wish upon a Star

Ask the person you love most
Three things they're wishing for
If one's a villa on the coast
Forget that, there's two more

The Idea: There's a wonderful organization named "Make a Wish" that makes dreams come true for kids with terminal illnesses. What a great way to say, "I love you." This idea is based on the same principle. Wouldn't it be nice if you could help make a wish come true for someone you love? Give it a try.

The genie in the lamp. Simply ask the one you love, "I'm curious to know what you would want if you were told you had three wishes?" To be creative, find an old lamp and give it to the one you love. Include a card with the above question. If he or she makes wishes that are not possible to fulfill, such as "I wish for ten million dollars" or "I wish for a life with no illness," ask him or her to think of things that are within reason.

You may want to respond by telling them three special wishes you would make and leave it at that. You wouldn't want the one you love to suspect your ulterior motives.

Your wish is my command. Your goal, how-ever, is to select one of the wishes and make it come true. If possible, try to make all three dreams come true. You may fall short because of your budget or other constraints. Just do your best.

For example, if one wish involves going to Hawaii some day, start a savings account especially for the trip. If Hawaii is out of the question, surprise the one you love some weekend by taking him or her to some place you can afford. You might say, "I couldn't make your Hawaii dream come true, but because I love you I wanted us to get away for a few days anyway. Keep dreaming. Some day your wish will come true."

13 ♥ Yuk, Yuk

If together you give
Lots of love and laughter
You just may live
Happily ever after

The Idea: Laughter is one of the more important ingredients to a lasting relationship. Find things to do with the one you love that make you laugh. When schedules get too busy or life is too stressful, find something to do that makes you both howl.

Laughing It Up: Below are some suggestions for tickling your funny bone.

>   *Rent your favorite comedy movie.* Go to your nearest video store and rent a movie that makes you both laugh. There's bound to be one or two movies that will tickle your funny bone time and time again.

>   *Get out or purchase your favorite funny book.* Books by humorists and gifted cartoonists abound. If you look hard enough, you will find one that parallels your sense of humor. When you find a book that makes you laugh, save it and share it with the one you love.

>   *Look at your old yearbooks* or old photographs. Seeing the way we looked years ago or read-

ing what someone wrote in our yearbook can often be the best entertainment around. Show someone who has only known you in recent years a picture that is ten, twenty, or thirty years old. If they don't laugh, they're probably being polite.

Go hear a comedian or two at a local comedy club or other place of entertainment near you. If there are no such places around, many professional comedians have made videos you can rent.

Just laugh! Sometime when you are sitting with someone you love or a group of people you love, just start laughing. Try to laugh harder and harder with each passing second. If two or more people begin laughing for no apparent reason, the laughter can become contagious. You may soon find yourself in a roomful of people who are laughing hysterically for no apparent reason. Keep it up. Few things are better for you than a good laugh.

14 ♥ Just Kidding

Find a carousel to ride
Or jump a rope instead
You can find the kid inside
It's all within your head

The Idea: Be kids for a day. Experience puppy love or that special camaraderie that is so characterized by childhood friendship. Do you become more dull and boring with each year? It doesn't have to be that way. Kids have ways of being and doing whatever they feel like at the moment. They seldom think, until they reach adolescence, "what will people say if I do this or that?" We as adults are all too concerned that someone may see us do "something childish." Why is that so bad?

Planning Your Day: Think of things little kids do that adults don't do very often. Observe your own kids, nieces and nephews, or grandchildren. See what playful things they do during a typical day. Then plan your day around childhood play. You may want to invite some children along to help you lose your inhibitions.

Selecting Activities:
- Build sandcastles.
- Run after the ice cream truck.
- Ride a merry-go-round.
- Visit a zoo.

- Play hopscotch or jump rope.
- Make drawings with crayons or water colors.
- Play with clay or Play-Doh.
- Roll down a hill.
- Visit a playground. Swing, go down the slide, get on the teeter-totter.
- Play hide and seek.

Making Your Day Even More Fun:

Try dressing up like little kids. Put your hair in pigtails or braids. Give everyone a lollipop or go out for an ice cream cone.

You may just discover old love can find youth again!

15 ❤ Home, Sweet Home

Why go out and run around?
Just stay at home alone
You control the mood and sound
Just disconnect the phone

The Idea: How many times have you put aside an evening together with someone you love, only to have it spoiled by a telephone call that changes your plans. This may be the most inexpensive and simplest idea in this entire book.

Setting the Stage: To enjoy your evening at home, you will need to do a little planning. Here are some things to consider.

> 1. If you and the one you love are husband and wife and you have children, find a babysitter who will take the children to her house. Instead of leaving the house to find some peace and quiet, you send away the noise and find peace and quiet within your own walls.

> 2. Set a specified time to get together. And stick to it. Don't let delays cut into your time at home together.

> 3. Decide that you and the one you love will

run all the errands and do all the chores that day before your specified meeting time. If anything didn't get done, you both agree to let it go for the evening.

4. Make a list of any supplies you might need. Food for the meal, if you're eating together. Wood for the fire. A new tape for the stereo.

5. Set the date with the one you love.

Making the Most of Your Evening:
Here are some additional ways to make the evening special.

1. UNPLUG YOUR PHONE. If the babysitter must have a telephone number, give your next door neighbor's (be sure your neighbor is home). He or she can alert you if there's an emergency. Aside from that, nothing should disturb your time together.

2. If the season is right and you have a fireplace, light a fire. Even if your companion for the evening is a child, a good friend, or a close relative, a fire adds warmth to the mood as well as to the room temperature.

3. Play some quiet music that will add to the serenity. For this particular evening leave the heavy metal music in the closet. Your purpose tonight is to talk, laugh, and enjoy each other.

4. Think of some activity you both enjoy do-

ing (other than watching television or a movie —these deter conversation).

5. Spend at least some time during the evening talking with each other. Take this planned opportunity at home to get to the heart of your love for each other. Evenings focused on someone else make that person feel special. And loved.

16 ♥ What Anniversary?

Celebrate times that are special to you
On the dates that would always be
*   missed*
The one thousandth day since you
*   first said "I do"*
Or the one hundredth time that you
*   kissed*

The Idea: Surprise the ones you love with special celebrations on days that will catch them completely off guard. Most of us remember anniversaries, birthdays, and other special events on the annual date that corresponds with the event's first occurrence.

For example, if your daughter was born on February 4, you always celebrate her birthday on February 4. But how can we surprise our loved ones with special days they are not even aware of?

Planning Special Surprises and Anniversaries: Here's how the idea works. Let's say Jim and Andrea were married on August 23, 1988. They would expect to celebrate their marriage on August 23 of every year thereafter. But what if on May 23, 1991, Jim were to come home with flowers, a gift, and an anniversary card. Andrea's first thought might be, "Jim forgot the month of our anniversary."

But Jim may be wiser than Andrea thinks! For Jim is actually celebrating the one-thousandth day since their wedding. Andrea had no idea that this milestone was coming. She is moved. And good old Jim is the greatest thing that ever happened, just because he sat down and made a few quick calculations.

The one-thousandth day celebration: In the above example, here's how we figured the approximate date.

Year one	365 days
Year two	365 days
Subtotal	730 days

Then we take the 730 and subtract it from 1,000 to see how many days into year three is the one-thousandth day.

1,000	days
−730	days
270	days

Next, if we figure there are an average of 30 days in each month, we divide the 270 days by 30 and arrive at a figure of exactly 9 months into year three. So if you add two years and nine months to the wedding date or any other significant event in your loved one's life, you will come within a few days of their 1,000th anniversary. Celebrate it!

If you've known the one you love a very long time, use similar steps to approximate your five-thousandth day together. Or your ten-thousandth!

Other Suggestions: Use the same idea for other events. If you are an employer and you love your employees enough, surprise them on the one-thousandth day since they joined the company. Here are a few other unusual days on which to surprise friends and loved ones:

- The seventh month (year), seventh day (month), and seventh hour (day) since you went on your first date with a special some-one.
- Plan a celebration of the first time your now-accomplished son or daughter, niece or nephew, played in a piano recital, joined Little League, or learned to read.
- Call an old school friend you haven't seen in five, ten, or even twenty years.

17 ♥ Complimentary Copy

Compliments don't come our way
Quite enough these days
Try to find the heart to say
"You're great" in many ways

The Idea: You can say "I love you" almost every time you see someone if you sincerely compliment him or her in some way. Compliments need not be directed only at appearance. People love to hear others say something nice about their sense of humor, work, or talents. Try to compliment the ones you love at least once a day.

Thinking about Compliments: You may want to affirm and compliment those you love in these areas:

- The way they dress
- Their genuine concern for others
- Their way of always making you laugh
- Their hospitality
- Their kindness
- Their sincerity
- Their cooking
- Their ability as mother
- Their ability as husband
- Their hair
- The outcome of some chore or project they completed

Turning the Tables: What about the times when you receive a compliment rather than giving one? Accepting kind words from people is another way to say you love them. By disagreeing with their compliments, you may be hurting their feelings. Learn to say thank you and give compliments in return. Have you ever caught yourself saying things like

> *"Thanks for washing the car.* [sarcastically] *I can't believe you took time out of your precious schedule to do it."*

Perhaps instead you could say,

> *"Thank you for washing the car. I don't think I've ever seen it look so good."*

When someone says, "You look so pretty today," do you say something like

> *"Oh stop. My hair's a mess, and my dress doesn't fit right."*

Perhaps instead you could say,

> *"Thank you, you're looking pretty fine yourself."*

In all your relationships with the people you love, work on encouraging their quality traits and on accepting the praise they give you in return.

18 ❤ A Day of Servanthood

*Stay with your loved one from
    morning 'til night
Do special things 'long the way
Then if you do well your loved one
    just might
Act as your servant some day*

The Idea: Designate a day when you will be your loved one's servant from the moment he or she wakes up in the morning until time to go to bed. You really have to be committed for this one. Think of all those things you do every day that you wish someone would do for you. Well, you will be fulfilling that wish for the one you love.

Items You Might Need: Although this day could take place without any props or additional items, you can have as much fun as you want with ideas such as these:

- Give the one you love a bell so he or she can ring it every time your services are needed.

- Find a maid or butler outfit and wear it throughout the day.

- Prepare a servant's kit filled with things like tissues (to clean glasses or to offer for their nose as needed), a pillow (so you can make the person comfortable when seated), or a glass (to keep by their side so you can offer sparkling water regularly). You could also plan to serve special refreshments throughout the day.

Planning Your Special Day of Servanthood: Tell the person in advance about the day so he or she can think about what to have you do. Or, if that idea scares you, simply tell the person to reserve the day for something special. You can reveal your servanthood status as you begin your day together.

Enjoying Yourselves: Have fun with this one. Don't limit your servanthood duties to the obvious, such as serving breakfast in bed or bringing in the morning paper. Think again about those daily chores *you* hate doing.

- How many men enjoy shaving? If the one you love is a man, shave him, barber style, that day. Organize his ties by colors or patterns. Shine his shoes.

- If the one you love is a woman, brush her hair. Give her a manicure. Polish her briefcase or mop the kitchen floor.

Going the Extra Mile:

- If you like the bell idea mentioned earlier and want to give a memento of the day, have the bell engraved with your loved one's name and the date.

- Invite others in your family or group to help you in your role of servant. The more people involved, the more fun you can have. (And the less work you'll have to do!)

- Crown the one you love as you begin your day. Make him or her feel like a king or queen, well deserving of your servanthood commitment.

- If he is the one who usually takes out the trash or she the one who always cleans the bathroom, extend your day of servanthood by saying you will do those chores each day or week for the next month.

19 ♥ I Do, I Do

Reenact your wedding day
Renew the vows you made
If you're single there's a way
To thank the friends who have stayed

The Idea: This idea might seem most appropriate for married people, but it can be altered to fit any relationship. We suggest you renew the vows you made to one another if you are married. If you are not married or you want to renew vows to family members or friends, we have provided suggestions for doing that.

Saying "I Do" Again: Many different times and circumstances call for a renewal or recognition of commitment to another person. Below are a few suggestions.

- *Renew your wedding vows every year on your anniversary.* This idea is great for those who are new in their marriage and may not have enough years under their belt to conduct a full reenactment of the ceremony. Try making a tradition of this event. Get out your wedding ceremony and recite the promises you made to each other on that first day God joined you together. It might help you refocus on priorities that have gotten cloudy.

- *Reenact your wedding day.* If you've been married for several years, pick your next major anniversary as the day you will reenact your wedding day. Perhaps you still live near the place where the wedding was held. Go there. If not, conduct the ceremony right in your own backyard or in your home. It doesn't have to be a fancy affair.

   The two of you may want to do this alone. Or you may want to include your immediate family. Invite the original wedding party if you like. If you're the type of person who likes to throw a party, invite everyone you know!

- *Renew your commitment to your children.* Parents can set aside a special day when each child is thirteen or sixteen or after high school graduation. You might share with the child your love and confess your shortcomings. Ask your child to forgive you for those times you have blown it.

- *Recognize close friends in a special way.* Perhaps you have no one with whom to renew vows, but you may have a few loyal friends whom you want to recognize. Issue them a Covenant of Friendship, and thereafter celebrate their friendship each year on the anniversary date of your promise. The document might look something like this:

A COVENANT OF FRIENDSHIP

Our world has ways of recognizing and celebrating marriages, births, and other family relationships. But few people take the opportunity to celebrate some of the most treasured
people in their lives: our best friends.

this certificate is presented to

[Nathan Valypoulos]

BY HIS FRIEND _____
ON THIS _____ DAY OF _____
NINETEEN HUNDRED AND NINETY _____

*I hereby covenant to be your friend
until the day I die.*

20 ♥ Flower Power

*Nothing's more simple, Nothing's
     more right
Than flowers delivered by you
Do it today; do it tonight
And do it one week, maybe two*

The Idea: For centuries the gift of flowers has been the most practical and sentimental way for one person to express his or her love for another. We send flowers for birthdays, anniversaries, or when a friend gets a promotion at work. We even send flowers during the tragic times of life. Whatever the occasion, the implied message is still, "I love you, and I'm thinking about you today."

Just watch a group of women in an office try to sit still when a delivery person brings in a bouquet of flowers. Almost every one of them will ask herself, "I wonder who they're for?" or "Who could be sending me flowers?" (Why do we use the example of women in an office receiving flowers? Because not enough women have made the move to send a man flowers!)

Using Flowers to Say "I Love You":

- The most obvious way of using flowers is to send a bouquet to your loved one's home or office. Delivering the flowers yourself is even more special because you are there to see your loved one's reaction.

- Consider bringing flowers home every night for one week.
- Take a walk with your loved one and pick wildflowers. Create your own bouquets.
- On special birthdays, use flowers in unique ways. For example, if it is your loved one's thirtieth birthday, have a different person present a rose and a special note every fifteen minutes throughout the day. Finally you arrive with rose number thirty.
- Send flowers to people in your office, friends, or church members who may never have received flowers before. Let them know they are loved too.
- Adopt a code using certain flowers. For example,

A rose means "I love you."

A daisy means "let's play."

A pansy means "I'm thinking about you."

A daffodil means "I'm sorry."

21 ❤ Prime Time

Try this one for seven days
Do not turn on the set
Use this book or your own ways
Make this your best week yet

The Idea: The reason television executives call evenings prime time is because this is the part of the day when most Americans are gathered around their television sets. What would happen if you, and everyone else in your house, promised to leave the television off for one full week? What are you going to do with all that time?

Why not spend it with the ones you love! Children spend as much time in a year in front of the television as they do in front of teachers. Many adults spend even more time than their kids in front of the set. So why not make time to talk, play, and listen to each other?

So Now What Do We Do? The following is a suggested schedule for your seven days without television.

Day 1: Take a walk together and plan what you're going to do with the time you would normally be watching television. If you have children, bring them along too. Let them be a part of the planning process.

Day 2: Play games together. If you don't like card games, then bring out the board games. Scrabble. Monopoly. Clue. Do a crossword puzzle together.

Day 3: Make a surprise visit to one of your close friends, perhaps a neighbor or someone you know who may need company.

Day 4: Build a fire in the fireplace or hold your own private barbecue in the backyard. Just spend time enjoying each other's company.

Day 5: Work together on some project around the house or run some errands that you need to get done. Be active.

Day 6: Turn to one of the other ideas in this book and say "I love you" in that way.

Day 7: Make this day a day of rest. Relax around the house, go to the park and lie in the grass, or visit the beach or a nearby lake. Then come home and just talk. Discuss with one another how much time you were able to spend together instead of watching TV. You'll soon realize how "prime" time can truly be!

22 ❤ Food for Thought

Focus a day 'round every meal
Eat breakfast, a lunch and a
dinner
We're not really sure how you will
feel
But it certainly won't be thinner

The Idea: Most of our socializing with the ones we love is done during mealtimes. This idea suggests that you take one full day and plan to have three very special meals with the one you love.

Planning the Venue: Good food is important, but the settings for your meals together need careful attention. Here are some suggestions.

Breakfast

- Serve breakfast in bed.
- Go to the place in town that serves the best brunch.
- Make waffles with a choice of a dozen different toppings.
- Buy Alpha Bits cereal and spell "I love you" on the plate or in the bowl.
- Eat breakfast at a place where you can enjoy the morning view.

Lunch

- Plan a picnic lunch and find a private spot at the beach or in the woods.
- Take the one you love out for lunch and have close friends waiting there to join you.
- Order pizza and have the cook spell "I love you" with pepperoni.

Dinner

- Find the most romantic place you can for dinner.
- Have a candlelight dinner at home.
- Have friends come over and serve you dressed like maids and butlers.
- Go out to your favorite restaurant.
- Splurge on dessert.
- Eat somewhere where you can watch the sunset.

An Added Note: In many households throughout the United States, families seldom eat one meal together in a week, let alone three meals together in a day. This way to say "I love you" could not only focus on one day with three special meals, but also on the suggestion that you try to eat meals with the one you love and members of your family as often as possible—even if it means reworking some schedules.

23 ♥ Gone Fishin'

Vacation time! Let's rant and rave
But where? That will depend
On how much money you can save
And how much you don't spend

The Idea: We all need time away from our daily routines to be with those we love. One of the best ways to tell someone that you love him or her is to plan a vacation together. Even if you don't have vacation time available in the immediate future, set the time now. Half the fun of a vacation is planning and anticipating a special trip.

Considering a Budget: You don't have to have an enormous budget to plan a vacation. In fact, some of the most relaxing vacations are those close enough to home so that travel costs are low, yet far enough away that you feel removed from everyday pressures.

If you don't have any money for a trip, set your vacation far enough in the future to allow time to save the money you'll need. Set a savings plan you can stick to.

Picking the Location: Gather together all the people who will be going on the trip. Next, keeping in mind the budget constraints you've already established, use a map to explore location possibilities.

If you are on a limited budget, you may just need a map of your state or the surrounding states. If you have a more generous budget, you may want a map of the United States. And if you are one of those rare people for whom money is no object, get out a map of the world.

Developing a Preliminary Plan: Together, complete a plan similar to the following outline. As the date of departure gets closer, you can give the plan more detail.

VACATION PLAN
for

_____

(list names here)

Date of Departure: _____   *Return:* _____

Destination:

_____

Mode of travel:

_____

Route:

_____

Lodging or camping accommodations needed:

_____

One activity each person would like to do during this trip:

Name	Activity for this trip
_____	_____
_____	_____
_____	_____
_____	_____
_____	_____
_____	_____
_____	_____
_____	_____

24 ♥ Write It Down

Grab some paper, grab a pen
Write a special note
Say you think that she's a "ten"
Or pin it to his coat

The Idea: Who can say they don't like getting a note from someone with the words *I love you* written on it. (Maybe some of you macho people out there don't think it's cool to *write* such a note. But admit it. How do you feel when someone sends *you* a note that says "I love you"?) For many people writing "I love you" is much easier than saying it.

Saying the "Write" Thing: Of course, the easiest thing to do would be to go to the stationery store and find a gushy, sentimental card designed for a special occasion. But don't wait for a special occasion. Try this idea on the spur of the moment.

Your goal for one particular day will be to find as many ways as possible to write the words, "I love you." Here are just a few suggestions to get you started.

- Write your I-love-you note on the mirror in the bathroom with toothpaste.
- Let the grass grow thick and tall and then mow the words I LOVE YOU with the lawnmower.

- Take the one you love to the beach and write "love letters" in the sand.
- Slip a note in the cereal box so that it comes out as the cereal is poured.
- Put a big "I love you" sign *inside* the refrigerator.
- Write "I love you" in bold black letters on the tenth sheet of your roll of toilet paper.
- Send an I-love-you note by registered mail to your loved one's office.
- Use a bar of soap to write "I love you" backwards on the rear windshield so that the words will read forward in the rearview mirror.
- Put notes in any items your loved one will open that day, such as a briefcase, purse or wallet, golf bag, schoolbook, or lunch box.
- Find an old pillowcase and write on it so that your loved one can end the day with a final "I love you."

- Some of Your Own Ideas:

_____

_____

_____

_____

_____

_____

_____

_____

_____

_____

_____

_____

_____

_____

_____

_____

25 ♥ A Little TLC

Treat your loved one kind
Buy her a corsage
Have his shoes all shined
And give them a massage

The Idea: Treat the one you love to some tender, loving care. Do this because you want your loved one to have a fun day taking care of him or herself for a change, instead of caring for everyone else.

Setting a Budget: At first glance this may seem like an expensive idea, but it doesn't have to be that way. You can go all out and buy him or her everything listed below, or you can accomplish a similar goal by doing only one or two of the ideas suggested. Maybe you and your loved one have a mutual friend who would help you do some of the suggestions listed below for free or for a minimal amount, just to share in making the day special for the one you love.

Planning to Pamper: You can do many things for the one you love to make this day of pampering an unforgettable experience. Here are just a few activities you can schedule for him or her.

- A haircut or time with a hairdresser
- A manicure
- A massage by a masseuse

- Time at the department store to buy a new dress or suit
- An hour in a hot tub
- A sauna
- A nap

An Alternative: Instead of (or in addition to) treating the one you love to the above pampering, make some changes in your own appearance. If you're walking around with tangled hair, a stringy goatee, or holes in your jeans, try having your own hair styled, your face shaved, or buying yourself a new pair of slacks. If your nails are chipped and you haven't worn a dress in more than a year, get a manicure and put on something that makes you look and feel pretty. Your loved one just might fall in love with you all over again!

26 ♥ Theme Dates

Pick a theme, then send a card
Plan three new dates or four
It helps to keep them off their guard
When surprises are in store

The Idea: This way to say "I love you" is great if you are planning a surprise for the one you love, and you want to catch him or her off guard.

Plan a series of three or four dates centered around a theme. (Some suggested themes are listed below.) If you have an event planned that you don't want the one you love to suspect, such as a surprise party, you can incorporate it into date number three or four of your series.

Planning Theme Dates: Let's say a guy named Doug sends his girlfriend Cindy a card inviting her to go on a series of dates the first Saturday of each month over a period of four months. The dates will be centered around the theme of transportation.

August date: Doug and Cindy board a train and travel two hours to a quaint town where they enjoy a walk in the country and a romantic dinner at sunset. At the end of the day, they board the train and return to their hometown.

September date: While the weather is still warm, the

two journey to a nearby river where a paddle boat takes people for afternoon trips and then back to their original port for a riverside barbecue.

October date: To view the brilliant colors of changing fall leaves in nearby mountains, Doug and Cindy drive to a local aerial tramway that goes up the side of a mountain. At the top the two find an open meadow and eat a picnic lunch.

November date: Bundled in their wool sweaters to keep warm, Doug surprises Cindy by driving his car up to an awaiting hot air balloon. The huge aircraft, now aloft, is silhouetted against the orange sunset. Cindy is caught completely off guard when Doug opens a small black velvet box, removes a ring, places it on Cindy's finger, and says, "Cindy, I love you. Will you marry me?"

Had Doug not already planned a series of fun dates prior to the hot air balloon ride, Cindy might have been a little suspicious. Coming at the end of a series of dates with a similar theme, he was able to surprise his loved one with a very special gift.

Considering Other Themes:

- *North, South, East, and West—Plan a series of short journeys to nearby spots in each direction.*
- *The Four Seasons—Regardless of the time of year, choose a spring, summer, fall, and winter event.*
- *High and Low—Within a hundred miles of your home, find the highest elevation, the lowest elevation, and two locations in-between. Plan activities as close to these sites as possible.*
- *Aquatics—Visit a lake, a stream, an ocean, and a waterfall.*

27 ♥ One Day at a Time

How do I love thee?
Let me count the ways
From deep down inside me
Some thoughts for all your days

The Idea: You may have seen popular calendars showing "a joke a day," "a proverb a day," or "a quote a day." Here's your chance to create the same kind of calendar for the one you love.

This project can be as simple as providing love thoughts for a week, or, if you want to take the time, you can make enough pages for a month. If you really want to impress your loved one, create a calendar with 365 pages! We recommend the month-long option.

Preparing Your Love-Thought-for-the-Day Gift: Begin by purchasing either a nice calendar or a bound journal with blank pages. These items should be available in most stationery stores.

If you are preparing enough pages in a small journal for one month, number each two-page layout with the days of the month (1st, 2nd, 3rd, and so on). Don't bother putting in the names of the days of the week. Your loved one may want to use this calendar again in future months.

Now, write a brief thought on each page about why you love this special person, or tell what you like best about him or her.

Getting Your Mind (Heart) in Gear— Some Examples:

- 9th. Your sense of humor is unmatched by anyone. You make me laugh as no one else can.

- 14th. I love how you encourage me when I'm down.

- 25th. It's this simple. I love you.

- 30th. Thanks for spending so much time with me.

Presenting Your Love-Thought-for-the-Day Calendar: Once your journal is completed, buy a card that suits the moment and give it to the one you love at dinner. Explain that he or she can only look at each page on the day indicated. No fair looking ahead.

28 ♥ Pick a Project

Pick a project you want done
One you hoped they'd do
It can't be one that seems like fun
Or by now they'd be through!

The Idea: What better way to tell someone of your love than to perform some awful or tedious task that has been hanging over him or her like a gray cloud. It may be a project that the one you love has wanted done for a long time.

For example, you can pull all those weeds that ruin the view from your loved one's window. You can replace or wash all the screens on the doors. You can clean out the garage or that hall closet that hasn't been touched since you moved into the house.

Below we have provided a worksheet to help you plan your project. You might want to do this on a day when the one you love isn't home. Then the completed project can be your surprise gift.

Special Project Worksheet

Step One—Pick a Project

List below all the projects he or she would like to have done but doesn't want to do.

_____

_____

_____

_____

Now circle the least pleasant one. That's what you're going to do first.

Step Two—List Your Supplies

List the paints, tools, do-it-yourself books, and other items you may need.

_____   _____

_____   _____

_____   _____

_____   _____

Step Three—Get to Work!

Ending the Day: Once you have finished your project, show the one you love all the work you have done. Explain that you did the task because you loved him or her so much you wanted to take away a burden.

29 ♥ Row, Row, Row Your Boat

Drop all those pencils
Forget the chores
Stow your utensils
And trade them for oars

The Idea: Find a lake resort within driving distance where a rowboat can be rented. Don't even think of renting a boat with an outboard motor. We're talking about love, not noise.

Making Your Day Special: Before you leave for your aquatic excursion, here are some suggestions to consider as you plan your special day.

1. *You might want to pack an ice chest.* Bring your loved one's favorite snacks and beverages to enjoy on the lake. Bring along some old bread or crackers to feed the ducks too. Just in case the seats are not comfortable (which goes almost without saying in rowboats), take along a couple of cushions.

2. *Pick your loved one's favorite time of day.* If he or she is a morning person, go as early in the day as possible, while the water is still and the sounds are distinct. If the one you love enjoys the outdoors, go at midday to bask in the sunshine. Then, there's late afternoon. Fewer people are around, and the sun is

low in the sky. Your loved one may enjoy a boat ride just before sunset.

3. *Find a spot that is away from the crowd.* Don't row your entire time together. Bring in the oars and enjoy the time with the one you love. The only sounds you should hear are the lapping of the water on the side of your rowboat, the movement of nearby ducks, and your conversation.

4. *Tell him or her how great it is to be together.* Then say, "I love you."

30 ♥ Habit Reforming

*Quit a bad habit for those in your
  life
Take all that booze off the shelf
Give up on smoking just for your
  wife
Or give it all up for yourself*

The Idea: This idea revolves around telling at least two people that you love them—your most significant loved one and yourself. Do you have a habit or mannerism that irritates those around you? Maybe it's something as serious as eating too much, or maybe it's as minor as snapping your chewing gum. In any case, bad habits may be adding stress to your relationships with those you love.

You can show those close to you how much you care about them by changing those idiosyncrasies or bad habits that bother them.

Giving Up For Love: Here are a few examples of habits many of us could consider ending.

- Tapping a pen on the table
- Leaving the seat up on the toilet
- Cussing
- Leaving lights on in the house
- Chewing with your mouth open
- Returning the car without fuel

Breaking the Habit: Some habits are tough to break. Others may be more simple than you think. No matter how bad your habit, there is hope for change. Others have changed. You can do it too!

If the habit that annoys the one you love is basically harmless, ask him or her to tell you nicely when you are doing it. You may not even know you are doing it. Then take action to change your behavior. Here are some suggestions:

- If your habit is snapping your chewing gum, practice chewing with your mouth shut. Or, don't chew gum when you are around the one who gets annoyed.
- If your habit is whistling the same song over and over again, try humming softly instead.
- If your habit is picking your teeth, carry a toothbrush around.

If the habit you want to change is more serious, seek the help you need. For example, there are a number of programs designed to help you stop smoking. There are also programs to help you overcome addictions to drugs, alcohol, or other chemicals. We both work for a place that can help you overcome tough problems or addictions. Call us at 800-227-LIFE for help.

31 ♥ A Way When Away

Absence makes the heart grow fonder
You may know it's true
So when they travel far and yonder
Make them fonder too

The Idea: There almost always comes a time in the lives of people who love one another when they are separated. Husbands and wives are sometimes separated due to business trips, family events, or even retreat time spent alone. Parents are often separated from their children for any number of reasons, including summer camp, visits to grandparents, and going off to college.

Once we reach adulthood, many of us live thousands of miles from loved ones and family. This way to say "I love you" keeps us in touch with the people we love, whether it's a two-day trip or a year away from them. Here are some suggestions. You can use as few or as many as you like.

Leaving Love: *When the one you love is going away*

- Put a little gift in his or her luggage.
- Prepare a care package with candy, mints, gum, a book, or of things to do on an airplane, bus, or train.
- If your loved one is going away for more than two or three days, prepare a set of

envelopes—one for each day he or she is gone. Put in each envelope a note, a photo of the two of you, and anything else that makes the one you love think of you.

When you are the one going away

- Call your loved one every day. Call more often if your budget permits.
- Leave a gift somewhere that will be found after you're gone.
- Make a cassette tape for the one you love to listen to while you're away.
- Call the ones you love and tell them you are going to watch a certain movie. Ask them to watch the same movie. Later you can talk about the movie as though you saw it together.

When the ones you love live far away

- Start calling them more often. If you usually call once a month, begin calling every other weekend. If you call once a week, begin calling twice a week.
- Drop a card telling them you miss them and love them. Assure your loved ones that you are doing well just knowing that they love you too.
- Instead of writing letters, record a cassette tape for them, telling them all about your

life. Not only is this easier than writing a note, they would probably love to hear your voice. Then ask them to send a tape back to you.

32 ♥ Once Upon a Time . . .

Before you say you cannot write
Let your mind go wild
Say "He's been my shining knight"
Or "She cooks like Julia Child"

The Idea: Most of us remember sitting down as little kids while an adult read from a book of fairy tales. Perhaps we most wanted to be like Cinderella, swept away from our dusty corner in the house to the fanciest ball in town. Or like Gulliver, we sought travel to faraway lands, visiting people much different from ourselves.

Now you can create a story of your own based on your relationship with the one you love. This idea is also appropriate for your entire family or any other group of friends or loved ones. Include as many people as you want in your story.

Preparing the Story: All you need is a pen, a pad of paper, and lots of imagination. You might try following these steps as well.

1. Go to your local library and wander through the children's books section. Sit down and read a few stories. Start with Dr. Seuss or stories by the Brothers Grimm.

2. Now, on separate pieces of paper, write down your name and the name of each loved one you want included in the story. Start listing the positive attributes about each person and some fun facts about their background.

3. Write your story by telling about your childhood and the childhood of the one you love. Talk about how you met. Explain your present situation. Let your mind go wild about the future. You might even use the ending: ". . . and they lived happily ever after."

A Sample Fairy Tale: Now, let's look at a fairy tale about a flight attendant from Tucson who met her Floridian contractor husband while they were in college at Notre Dame. (The story is written as if a husband wrote it for his wife.)

Once upon a time there was a cute little princess named Cathy who lived in the desert. Her long blonde hair was shiny and soft. Her eyes were as blue as the sky. She and her two sisters often walked through the desert picking wildflowers.

Far away, in another land near a great ocean, a little prince ran with his new puppy along the shoreline. An only child, Billy hoped one day to find a very special friend.

Cathy grew to be a pretty young woman and went to a land called Indiana to further her education. Meanwhile, Billy decided to attend college in the same land. One day when the air outside was crisp and snow was falling, Billy saw Cathy warming her hands near the fire in the student lounge. She was so pretty, in her soft pink sweater and winter coat. He had never seen anyone so beautiful before. He knew then that she was the special friend he had always wanted.

Cathy and Billy became friends, married, and flew away on a cloud. He builds gingerbread houses in meadows. She sails high above the Earth on the wings of a big silver eagle.

Every morning when Prince Billy awakens, he gazes at his princess and thanks God for his special gift. As they journey into the future, they gaze ahead at the hillsides covered with blue and red flowers. Above the rolling hills before them are the words "Billy Loves Cathy" written in the sky.

The Big Day: Once your story is completed and you feel good about it, set a date with the one you love. Find a location that has some relationship to your story, the flowered hillside, the desert plain. Take him or her there. Sit down together and read the story.

Going a Step Further: If you really want to impress the one you love, here are some ideas to make your fairy tale even more fun.

- Have someone you know do illustrations for the story.
- Wear a goofy costume that will add some humor.
- Bring objects mentioned in your story.
- Have your story printed and bound to make a memento the one you love will always cherish.

33 ♥ Adoption Papers

Give a gift or plant a tree
Adopt for them a bear
You can help the Earth you see
And tell loved ones you care

The Idea: You can tell someone you love him or her by doing good deeds. If the one you love has a special interest in some cause, has actively volunteered for a charity, or has spent time trying to save a part of our Earth, show him or her that you support that interest.

Saying "I Love You" by Giving to Others or Adopting a Cause: There are a variety of ways you can help the Earth, your city, the local environment, or unfortunate people while at the same time telling someone, "I love you."

> *Plant a tree.* Find a place in your city where you can plant a tree in the name of the one you love. Many cities allow this in community parks or along public roads. (You could even plant a tree for each member of your family.) Then, occasionally, you can go by to see how much the tree has grown. If you can't find a public place to plant a tree, do it in your own backyard.
>
> *Adopt an animal.* Most city zoos today have a

program where you can adopt one of their animals by making a donation or by becoming a "friend of the zoo." If the one you love loves animals, this might be an appropriate thing to do.

Donate to charity. If the one you love is active in some charity, make a special contribution to that charity in his or her name. You might even be able to take up a collection from friends and tell your loved one that the total donation will be dedicated to that special work.

Adopt a highway. Some cities, counties, or states allow you to adopt a segment of a highway. If there is no such program near you, you can get one started and designate the one you love as the adopter. You can visit that stretch of highway, and do your part to make sure it is free of litter.

Contribute to a building project. Often community theaters, churches, university buildings, and other public-oriented buildings under construction are projects that need people to donate in various amounts. You may be able to donate enough to dedicate a seat in the local community playhouse in the name of the one you love.

34 ♥ True Blue

No better way to show you care
Than when they're down and out
Find some time of yours to share
That's what love's all about

The Idea: Everyone has had a bad day. Some of us have even had bad weeks! There is no time in a person's life when he or she needs to feel loved more than when the gray clouds appear. Usually there are reasons why we become depressed.

- Someone close to us has moved away, and we miss this special person.
- We just had a rotten day at work.
- A loved one is ill.
- We just feel lonely.

Sometimes we can't explain what's wrong. We just have the blues.

Taking Away the Blues: Some people try to make their loved ones laugh their pain away. If that works for the one you love, give it a try. The laughter you create may be just the sunshine needed to break through some of the clouds. But if you are not able to humor the one you love out of the blues, try some of these simple ideas.

Just sit with them. Many of us are so uncomfortable when someone is depressed that we flee. We may feel like we must keep talking to lessen our own anxiety, or we may feel compelled to offer solutions that we know won't work. But someone who really feels blue usually doesn't want to hear half-baked solutions. That person just needs us to be there. Don't try to "fix" anything. Just be there.

Listen. If you sit with the person long enough, he or she may be able to talk to you. Often, a person with the blues just needs someone to hear his or her woes. Even if the situation doesn't sound so bad to you, it's certainly important to the person who's depressed. Be nearby and ready to listen.

Affirm your love. The best help we can sometimes give a friend or loved one who is hurting is the affirmation that he or she is worth our love. Let the person know you care. Let him or her know you will be there to help.

Hug them. There are people around you every day who may not have received a hug for months. If there's a person in your life who is hurting, try giving him or her a hug.

35 ♥ This Is Your Life

Send them back and make them sob
With those who meant the most
Monty Hall will need a job
For you're a game show host

The Idea: Anyone born before 1960 should remember the television show in which Ralph Edwards would surprise and honor someone on stage. Various people who had been a part of the honored person's life would appear from behind a curtain and share a personal story. You can provide the same kind of adventure for the one you love. (Here's your chance to find out what Pammy Sue, his old high school sweetheart, is really like. Track her down and invite her—if you dare.)

It is probably best to keep this idea a surprise. If your loved one knows in advance that you are planning a "This-Is-Your-Life" event, much of the excitement will be taken away. Granted, this idea is a little more time-consuming than some others in this book, but you can do a simplified version and have just as much fun.

Preparing for the Big Night: Although you could hold this event during the day, it might be more appropriate in the evening. Most of your preparation for this particular idea will take place prior to the Big Night. This event will be least expensive and most successful if you apply it to a loved one who is living close to where his or her roots are. Or, if you and the one you love are planning a trip to your loved one's hometown, perhaps you can plan ahead and have this event happen while he or she is "home."

- First, clear a date about two months in advance with the one you love. You're going to need some time to implement your plan.

- Go through your loved one's old pictures, scrapbooks, or other nostalgic items. As you find people who have been influential in your loved one's life, write down their names. You might also ask your loved one's family members if they have any names to suggest or if they think the names you have are good ones. If you are applying this idea to someone you grew up with, this step should be quite easy for you.

- Track down as many of the people on your list as you can. Ask them if they are available and if they would be willing to be a part of this special evening.

- Begin preparing your script. Find out a tidbit of relevant information that was unique to each person's relationship with the one you love. Think of something appropriate to say and something appropriate for each person to say before appearing "on stage."

- Select a location. You may want to invite all of your loved one's friends. Or you may want to make this an intimate event with only close family and friends. Whatever you decide, pick your location accordingly. It can be as simple as a friend's home or as elaborate as a banquet room at a nearby hotel.

Staging the Big Night: You should make sure that all the surprise guests arrive well before the scheduled arrival of the one you love. Put them in a room located behind the place where the guest of honor will sit. When the guest of honor appears, have everyone in the "audience" say, THIS IS YOUR LIFE! Once the one you love has gotten over the shock and embarrassment of such a greeting, tell him or her not to turn around at any time. Then, bring on your first guest.

Making the Night More Memorable:
Here are a few items that can make the special night a living memory that will last forever.

- In keeping with the original "This Is Your Life" program, make up a scrapbook for the evening. A photo of each surprise guest could be featured. A handwritten message expressing personal sentiments can be placed next to each photo.

- Have a banner hanging above the chair where the guest of honor will be seated.
- After the last surprise guest is introduced, allow your loved one to say a few words.

36 ♥ Roast the Turkey

Gather friends who mean the most
Tell them to prepare
For a very special roast
But do it all with care

The Idea: You have probably seen a celebrity on television "roasted" by his or her peers. A roast is an event where one person is honored through a series of presentations or speeches by his or her friends, family, coworkers, or others. Each speaker takes a turn poking fun at the personality traits or life experiences of the honoree. Usually, a roast occurs as part of an evening dinner party.

We suggest you do the same for the one you love. You don't need to rent a banquet room at the local hotel. Keep it simple. Hold a dinner at your home and invite some of your closest friends.

Comedian Don Rickles used to be the king of roasts. His jokes and barbs were quite direct. However, we suggest you use sensitivity when implementing this idea for the one you love. Remember, the intention is to have the guest of honor laughing *with* the audience.

Selecting Your Presenters: At least a week before your roast, make a list of all those people you think should be presenters. Select a good cross section of the people who are part of your loved one's life. For example, pick one or two coworkers, a couple of clever family members, someone from church, a neighbor, and an old high school friend.

Providing Suggestions for the Presenters:
You might want to give each presenter an assigned topic based on their relationship to the one you love. For example, Nick, a successful yet compulsive executive, might be roasted by the following people.

> *His boss* may be asked to "roast" his behavior at work: Nick is a "detail man." He would know if someone had been sitting at his desk by checking to see if one of the ten pencils in his drawer had been used without being resharpened.
>
> *His golfing buddy* may be asked about his golf game: Nick is the only guy I know that walks off the golf course with more golf balls than he brought. He spends more time collecting balls others have lost than he does playing the game. Nick, have you ever purchased a golf ball in your life?
>
> *A fellow elder at church* may be asked to explain Nick's behavior in a board meeting: We can always rely on Nick to make sure the minutes of the last meeting are correct. Not only does he take his own notes to keep track of each detail, he corrects the spelling and grammar of everything that's passed out.

Affirming the Roastee: Since you are trying to show the one you love how much he or she is
loved, be sure each speaker ends with some words of
affirmation and encouragement. It's fun to laugh at
our own idiosyncrasies, but it's better yet to receive
praise for our quirks and foibles that are endearing to
others.

37 ❤ Money Is No Object

Go off on a shopping spree
Bring along your honey
Get the best gift there could be
'Cause you will spend no money

The Idea: One way to say "I love you" is to go on a shopping spree and buy the one you love as many gifts as possible. But since most people don't have enough money to do that, this suggestion is a little different. You're still going on a shopping spree with the one you love—you just aren't going to spend any money.

Outlining Your Day: Your goal for the day is to explore a series of shops together. Once you are in a store, go your separate ways, each of you searching for the perfect gift for the other (regardless of the cost).

    Then, when you have rejoined one another, show your loved one the gift you have selected. Let your loved one show you the gift he or she selected for you. Put both of the items back and leave the store. This kind of shopping doesn't cost you a dime, and you'll have loads of fun finding the perfect gift. Here are a couple of examples of how to shop when "money is no object."

    The card shop. Search high and low for the card that describes your feelings for the one you love. Once you've found the card, show it to him or her. Let your loved one read it, and then put it back. If you had fun finding the first card, you may want to search for several more.

The department store. You can do this kind of shopping one department at a time. Find the perfect suit, shirt, tie, and shoes for him. Find the right dress, scarf, accessories, and pumps for her. Then go to the jewelry department and then perfumes. Share your discoveries with the one you love.

You might also go into a pet store and find the pet you'd most like to give the one you love. Or go into a furniture store and select the piece of furniture you'd most like to give him or her.

(A hint to make sure you really follow the rules: Leave the cash, credit cards, and checkbook at home!)

Making the Most of This Idea: The primary benefit of this idea is that you and the one you love will be spending another fun-filled afternoon or evening together. Plus, you may find out some great ideas for upcoming birthday or Christmas gifts. So take along your notepad. It might come in handy.

38 ❤ Book Ends

Get a book, their favorite one
You can leather bind it
But do some more, for you're not
*   done*
Until the author's signed it

The Idea: Perhaps one of the people in your life loves to read. Even if the one closest to you doesn't read much, he or she probably has a favorite book. Here's your chance to give a special surprise, just to say "I love you."

Making Their Favorite Book a Special Gift: Below we have provided several suggestions of how you can use something as simple as a favorite book and make it a special and treasured gift.

>*First Edition.* If your loved one's favorite book is old, search used bookstores in your area on the chance that they may have a first or second printing copy. If you can't find a copy locally, ask a bookstore manager who carries rare books if he or she can direct you to a service that helps people find out-of-print and first edition books.
>
>*Leather Bound.* Even if you can't find an original issue of the favorite book, you can take a more recently published copy and have it professionally bound in a nice-looking, long-lasting leather cover.

Personalized. Write a very special and personal message on the inside cover of the book. Be sure to say "I love you" somewhere in that message.

Autographed. If the author of the book is still living, do whatever you can to have him or her sign your first edition or leather-bound copy of the book. You may want to send the book to them via certified mail, providing a shipping box and enough postage to return it to you. (Just in case this book becomes the favorite book of the one you love, we have autographed it for you below.)

39 ❤ Auto Mate

*Some day before they leave in the
  morn
Do crazy things to their car
Make other drivers lean on their
  horn
And tell them how in love you are*

The Idea: Before the one you love leaves for
work one morning, decorate the car as someone
might decorate a wedding car. This will be your special way of declaring your love publicly.

Preparing the Car: Below we have given
just a few examples of what you can do to your loved
one's car to let him or her—and the world—know of
your love.

- *Place signs on the car.* Say things like
  "Mike loves Debra" or "Annie loves Al-
  len." Put one on the back of the car that
  says "Linda loves Vince. Honk if you love
  someone today too!"
- *Put things inside the car.* Try filling every
  square inch of the backseat with colorful
  balloons.
- *Put a cassette tape in the car.* Record a message telling your loved one how much you
  love him or her.
- *Give your loved one some treats.* Put his or

her favorite candy, cookie, or munchie in the seat.

- *Write him or her a note.* Tell your loved one that you will clean up the car when he or she gets home.

40 ♥ Top 40

Choose some songs, your favorite hits
From "Sunny" to "Stormy Weather"
Act as DJ, use your wits
Then put it all together

The Idea: Music is one way people have been saying "I love you" for centuries. If you're a sentimentalist at all, you should know some songs that really set the mood for love. If you don't know who your loved one's favorite singer or musician is, find out.

Making Musical Memories: Here are a few suggestions of how you can use music with your loved ones. Some are very simple; others may take some time to prepare.

> *Make a tape.* If you and the one you love have known each other for a few years, you probably know some songs that bring special meaning to your relationship. Gather these songs together and record them on one tape using a home stereo system. You may want to add a narrative before each song, describing the setting where you first heard it. This idea would be especially appropriate for two old friends getting together after many years. For example, if you graduated from high school in 1968, gather some songs from that year. Play

the tape while you are together just to make your day even more nostalgic. (If you do not have the equipment or songs to make a tape on your own, many major record stores can make a custom tape for you incorporating almost any song you choose.)

Attend a musical play or movie together. Find a local community theater or a major performing arts center near you and attend a musical —especially if it is a love story. May we recommend an old Rodgers and Hammerstein musical such as "Carousel" or "The Sound of Music"? Buy the soundtrack in advance, and you can listen to the love songs on your way home.

Write a love song. While this idea is not appropriate for everyone, there are people who can write music for those they love. If you have no musical talent, rewrite the lyrics of a song specifically for the one you love. To make it fun, take a tune such as the theme song from an old television show like "Gilligan's Island," and substitute a story about yourself and the one you love.

Go to a concert. Find out your loved one's favorite musical performer. Even if you like rock and roll and his favorite singer is a country western star, go ahead and get the tickets. You might just enjoy yourself too.

Buy a tape. If there are no concerts near your city, or if her favorite performer is not coming to town, buy her a tape, album, or disc of her favorite group.

If none of our suggestions appeal to you, just get in the car, turn on some music, and sing your favorite songs together.

41 ❤ A Thousand Words

Van Gogh was quite an artist
From sunflowers to oceans
Now you can try your hardest
To paint from your emotions

The Idea: They say a picture is worth a thousand words. Have you ever been with someone and analyzed some great piece of art? You might have looked closely at the artist's technique and tried to figure out what prompted him or her to create that particular work.

Psychologists do much the same thing with the drawings of little children. Often the setting and actions depicted by children can inform professionals of the innermost thoughts a child may have. As adults we can do the same expressive artwork we did as children in order to show the love we have for others.

Making Art Work: This idea involves an activity you and the one you love can do together. Using one of the ideas listed below, set aside two or three hours for the sole purpose of creating a piece of art for the one you love. Work in the same location but completely independent of one another.

After purchasing your art supplies, begin simply by saying something like this: "In the next two hours I am going to do my best to create a painting that expresses my love for you. I am asking you to do the same. It doesn't have to be attractive or make sense to anyone else. When we're done, we're going to explain why we painted what we did for one another."

Selecting a Happy Medium: There are virtually an unlimited variety of art materials you could use for this activity. Here are a few of the more simple suggestions you could implement.

> *Oil Painting*—Buy two medium-sized blank canvas boards, a set of oil paints, and a few brushes. Share the paints, but don't look at each other's work until it's finished.

> *Water Colors*—Perhaps the easiest medium to use is water colors. You can buy water colors relatively inexpensively. And unlike the oil painting, which requires a canvas, water colors can be done on art paper.

> *Finger Paints*—Regress to childhood and create your picture using colorful finger paints.

> *Pastels or Pencil Sketching*—Some people may find pastels or pencil drawings easier to do than any type of paint.

> *Clay*—Use some Play-Doh or other flexible clay to sculpt a series of objects that tell a story during your sharing time.

Crayons—There is nothing wrong with making this activity simple. Each of you can sit down with a box of crayons. That's how we told stories as little kids. Why not do it again!

Giving an Art Show:

When you and the one you love have finished creating your works of art, show each other what you have created. Explain what it means to you. Then, prop up your creations. Sit back and start a thousand-word conversation. What do you see in your loved one's creation that he or she might not even realize is there? What further insights do you each have about your drawings, paintings, or other creations?

42 ♥ Extra! Extra!

Start the presses! Beat the deadlines!
No more morning blues
Let your loved one read the headlines
Now they're front page news!

The Idea: Imagine getting up in the morning and shuffling to the front door to get the morning paper. The brisk air chills your bones, you yawn as you close the door, and then you open the paper and see your name in headlines:

_____ **NAMED**

THE MOST LOVABLE PERSON IN TOWN!

As you read on, you find out that all the articles on the front page are love notes just for you. Your day has brightened. You seem to glide on air as you prepare your morning cup of coffee.

Acting as Editor and Publisher: You may not be able to print a newspaper front page that would look just like your local paper, but you can create a mock front page filled with articles about the one you love.

Before any newspaper can be printed, a publisher needs a team of talented writers and reporters. He or she also needs a means of printing the paper. In case you have no experience in such endeavors, here are some simple steps to follow in creating this "special edition."

1. Decide what topics should be covered in your newspaper. Perhaps you'll want to get out a copy of your local paper and thumb through the various sections to get some ideas.

Main news—Make this the article where you tell about this special-edition newspaper honoring the most lovable person in town.

Comics—Have a friend or family member write a funny story about your loved one's sense of humor. Get an illustrator, if you can.

Editorial—Have someone write a tongue-in-cheek opinion article answering a question like: "Why Everyone Should Be as Lovable as _____"

Sports section—Have a friend who golfs with your loved one write an article about his or her ever-improving golf game.

Life section—Honor the one you love by having someone do a feature article about his or her life.

2. Select a group of reporters and assign a deadline of about ten days from the date you give them the project. Ask each to write no more than one-and-a-half pages, double spaced. Your reporters can include family members and friends. For instance, if you do this for your husband on Father's Day, you could have your children write stories and draw pictures featuring Dad.

3. Once you have received your manuscripts from the various reporters (or once you are done writing the articles yourself if you are working alone), read through each article, making sure that they will be uplifting and fun for the one you love.

4. Now get creative. Write the headlines. The headline of a newspaper is the most important feature because it must draw attention to a story in just a few words.

5. After the articles have been written and edited, the headlines composed, and any photos or illustrations gathered, it's time to go to print. At one extreme, you can take your articles and headlines to a local typesetter and have them typeset in newspaper format, or you can have a local paste-up artist lay out your newspaper and make it ready for printing. Be sure to give bylines for those who contributed articles.

At the other extreme, you can get a blank sheet of newsprint-sized paper and hand print all of your articles. You can compromise somewhere between these two extremes by typing the articles on a standard typewriter and then pasting them to your paper. Of course, if you have access to desktop publishing equipment and software, you can produce a very professional-looking paper. Don't feel bad if you cannot have your paper typeset. Chances are the more simple and handmade the paper looks, the more it will be cherished.

6. Finally, it is time to distribute your paper. You may want to fold it inside a real newspaper to make sure the one you love sees it. Or you may simply want to hand over your front page and say, "Have you read the paper today?"

43 ♥ Movie Mania

Find a movie house near you
Pick a film that's right
See a matinee at two
Or drive-in late at night

The Idea: Take the one you love to a movie, but don't just go on Friday or Saturday night. Use one of the creative suggestions below to make the outing more fun, out of the ordinary, or romantic.

Getting Out of the Rut: Maybe you always go to the movies at the same theater. Maybe you go to the theater only on certain nights. Maybe you see the same kind of movie every time you go. Try adding a little variety to your life. Perhaps one of the ideas below will change your movie-going habits and create a new way of saying "I love you."

> *Go to a drive-in.* Going to a drive-in is something we all did as children but don't do very often as adults. There are many advantages to going to drive-ins, if you really think about it. You don't have to worry about how you look because the only people seeing you are the people going to the movie with you. A drive-in movie can also be more appropriate if you want to talk with each other during the movie. Still another advantage of the drive-in is the

fact that you can take lots of the people you love with you. Just borrow someone's van.

Go to a matinee. Some Saturday afternoon, drop everything, lock the doors, and find a movie you've wanted to see. If you live in a busy city where at night there are lines for the best movies, you can probably avoid the crowd by attending a matinee. When you leave the theater the sun will still be out! That will give you enough time in the day to find another way to say "I love you."

Rent a movie. If you have a VCR in your home, go to the video rental store and find a movie you both love. On the way home, buy some popcorn and your favorite beverage. Relax at home where you are most comfortable.

Go to an old movie. In some cities there are theaters that run old movies. If you have never seen some of the classics such as "Casablanca" or "Gone with the Wind" or "The Thirty-nine Steps," see one of these with the one you love.

Go to an old theater. Even though most of us are spoiled today with modern theater stereo systems, comfortable chairs, and air conditioning, there is something nostalgic about finding the oldest theater in your area and going to a movie there.

Have your own film festival. Select several film classics now on video and watch them during one evening or weekend with people who share your love of, say, the Marx brothers, W. C. Fields, or Marilyn Monroe. Your public library may have these films for loan.

44 ❤ Clowning Around

Put on a wig, paint your nose
Wear a funny shoe
Find a clown and rent his clothes
Don't let them know that it's you

The Idea: Do something hilariously funny to catch the one you love off guard. On some ordinary day, dress as a clown and gather a bouquet of balloons bearing the words "I love you."

Disguised in your festive garb, walk in to the place where the one you love works (or some other place where he or she will be) and present the balloons with a card signed by you. If your disguise is good, the one you love will think you've hired someone to deliver the balloons. When he or she finds out who the clown is, the surprise will be twice the fun.

Preparing in Advance: This idea will take some planning because you must arrange to rent, borrow, or make a clown suit, buy the makeup, and figure out when and where to spring the surprise. It might be a good idea if you notified your loved one's boss in advance, if you plan to deliver the balloons during a working day.

Other Costume Ideas—If a clown is not your style, go to a costume shop and look around. You might also consider one of the following:

- Rent a gorilla suit and bring bananas that say "I love you."
- Dress up as the Easter Bunny and deliver an Easter basket.
- Dress up as Santa and deliver some gifts.
- Dress up in Hawaiian attire and deliver leis.

45 ❤ Lights, Camera, Action

Though you do not work out at
*   Disney or Warner*
Someday that may be correct
You may see your star on some
*   Hollywood corner*
From making a film you'll direct

The Idea: Home movies have come a long way. Back in the sixties we'd have to wait weeks or months for Dad to use up the film, have it developed, rent a projector, and then find a wall large and white enough to double as a screen. And then, we'd see a scratchy film showing unrecognizable people.

Today you can use a home video camera, shoot an event, and then run into the house for all present to view *and* hear. Now you can show your loved one how much he or she is loved by secretly filming a movie starring all the loved ones in his or her life.

Obtaining Your Equipment: Although home video cameras are becoming a possession almost as common as microwave ovens, many people do not yet have one. If you don't have a friend who will lend a video camera to you, one can be rented from a camera store.

Preparing Your Production: Try to keep your video project fun, meaningful, and memorable for all involved. In each of the ideas listed below you have the option of preparing a detailed script or simply ad-libbing the whole show.

Have close friends be the "stars" of your production. Because your film is meant to be a surprise, have someone dress up as the one you love, and feature him or her as the leading man or woman.

Selecting Your Format: Here are some suggested formats for you to consider. You may have some ideas of your own.

> *"A Day in the Life of_____"*—Narration by the camera operator: "Meet _____. Here he is coming out of the front door of his lovely home. This is his wife. Together they have brought into the world four precious sons shown here playing flag football on the front lawn."

> *Create an evening news program*—Assemble a simplified set using a table and backdrop. Have each person in your cast serve as various newscasters. Report the latest news about your loved one's work, family, and friends.

> *Produce a series of television commercials*— This may be the easiest idea yet. Take a

photo of your loved one and place it on the front of an old mayonnaise jar. Have ten friends hold up the jar explaining why they would recommend your loved one to anyone. They might say, "He's the best friend I ever had." "He encourages me when I'm down." "He's the most helpful coworker in our office." "I would recommend this product to anyone who's looking for a friend."

46 ♥ A Friend in Need

When helping one who's lonely
Or someone who is blue
Bring your one and only
And they'll feel better too

The Idea: Somehow when we do things for other people out of an act of love, we receive even more love in return. Have you and the one you love ever spent some time with a hungry person? Have you ever visited a lonely person in prison? Why not multiply the love in your own hearts by sharing it with someone who may not feel loved at all?

Selecting the One in Need: Finding someone to serve should not be difficult. And there are hundreds of ways you could help a person who is hurting. We've listed a few ideas to get you started.

The homeless—There are thousands of homeless men, women, and children in America. Not all homeless people are mentally ill or alcoholics. Many are people like you or me who have fallen onto tough times. Call your local rescue mission or the International Union of Gospel Missions in Kansas City, Missouri, to see how you can help.

The lonely—Without even calling a service organization in town you may be able to think of a friend, someone at work, or a member of your church who would appreciate your company. Invite him or her over to dinner. Take him or her to the movies with you. Sit and listen to the person talk. Your presence can make the day seem brighter.

The prisoner—There are many organizations such as Prison Fellowship who are looking for people to visit and assist those serving time in prison. Find out what you can do to help.

The children—Consider sponsoring a child in a poor nation through organizations like World Vision. Together you and your loved one can write letters of encouragement and friendship to a little person you probably will never meet. Or, you can sign up to participate in a local Big Brothers/Big Sisters program and help a child in your own town.

47 ❤ Ad Vantage

Create yourself an ad campaign
Come on now, what the heck
You may do well and hired to train
An agency exec

The Idea: Write an ad campaign? You won't need to create ad copy that will be featured on Madison Avenue or create a famous jingle. Just use the various media that are around you on a daily basis to create an ad campaign implementing the theme, "[Carolyn] loves you."

Make your campaign last a day, a week, or an entire month. To keep it simple you may want to use one or two of the ideas suggested below throughout the year.

Advertising Your Love: Try these simple suggestions.

Method of advertising   *Your campaign*

Billboard

Stand on a street corner where you know the one you love will be driving by and hold up a large sign displaying your slogan, [ROB] LOVES [DINA]. Take it a step further and have several people do this on corners along your loved one's route home from work. Make your own personalized [SALLY] LOVES [STEVE] bumper sticker.

Radio	If you can't create your own radio ad, call up a radio station and request a song for your loved one. Pick a special song and ask the DJ to say something like, "This song is dedicated to a very special couple in San Pedro. Rob wants to let you know how much he loves you, Dina."
Television	Cut out a piece of paper the size of your television screen. Write across it in large, bold letters, "I love you." You may want to paste a picture of the two of you on the paper too. Then attach it to the front of your television.
Direct mail	Direct mail advertising includes those letters you receive in the mail daily from unknown solicitors. Simply take an envelope and make it

	look like the personalized direct mail you receive. Inside, simply write the words: I love [Tom].
Magazine ads	Get her a copy of her favorite magazine. Over one of the existing full-page advertisements, paste a sheet of paper that simply has the I-love-you words from your campaign.
Newspaper ads	Buy space in a local newspaper and run your own ad telling the one you love how much you care for him or her.

Perhaps you can think of more ideas as you are bombarded daily with advertisements. You can alter the above ideas to honor a son or daughter or to congratulate a colleague for a job well done.

48 ♥ An Advent Sure

During the month of December
Create some more joy each day
Make it a month to remember
With a calendar done in **your** *way*

The Idea: Some of the best activities from childhood are forgotten in adulthood, like having an Advent calendar at Christmas. Most of us probably don't get such a calendar any more unless there are children in the house. This idea allows you to create a special calendar for the one you love.

Creating Your I-Love-You Calendar:
Since we want to keep this project as simple as possible, we suggest you start with a store-bought Advent calendar. You can buy one for next to nothing right after Christmas.

Most of these calendars are created by gluing two sheets of paper together. The front page of heavier paper contains the windows that are opened. The thinner paper on the back has the pictures placed to show through the windows.

Carefully remove that back page. Then, in each location where a drawing is found, place a special message or photo that will bring joy to the one you love as he or she opens each window throughout the month. If you cannot remove the back sheet, open each window and paste your object over the existing picture. Close the windows and seal them with a small piece of tape or a small adhesive dot.

Selecting Items for Your Windows:
Here are a few ideas for the windows of your calendar.

- Photos of you and the one you love
- Photos of children or mutual friends
- Directions that might say, "Look under your bed" (hide a gift in that location)
- One- or two-word messages that are meaningful for the two of you

49 ♥ Camera Sly

Using photos from your past
And captions you have written
Give a memory that will last
When older you'll be gettin'

The Idea: There are many ways you can use photos to say "I love you." Grandchildren give them to grandparents all the time. We take pictures when we graduate from high school, when we get married, and when the first child is born. Why not use celluloid sentimentality to your best advantage? Here are some ideas:

Create a scrapbook of your times together. Trace your relationship with your loved one back to the time it began. If you have loved this person for any length of time, you probably have collected some pictures over the months or years. Take those pictures, put them in a scrapbook, and write your own captions for each. Make some comments sentimental and others humorous. Present the scrapbook to your loved one and go through it together.

Create a scrapbook of your childhood or your loved one's. Find either your baby pictures or your loved one's and make a scrapbook. Make up captions like, "Here you are wearing your mother's high-heeled shoes at the age of nine. You looked pretty then and you look pretty now!" Or, "Jeff at twelve. He was so tall, the coach asked him to put new nets on the basketball hoops. Nice legs!"

Make a poster. Take one of your favorite pictures of the two of you; have it blown up into a poster with a message like "Scott loves Jenny."

Have a portrait taken. If your budget will handle the expense, go out and have a nice portrait made of you and the one you love. Or, give him or her a certificate to have a portrait taken alone.

Frame your favorites. If the one you love has some favorite photos of you and the others he or she loves, have some of them framed and give them as a surprise gift.

Send them off. If you have parents, children, grandparents, or other loved ones who live in various parts of the country or world, send them pictures of you and those in your life regularly. Make them feel that they are a part of the activities and changes in your life.

50 ❤ Fa La La La La La La La La

Chestnuts roasting on an open fire
Shop before the stores all close
Yuletide carols sung with those you
*   admire*
And gifts wrapped up in pretty
*   bows*

The Idea: Ah, Christmas time. What better season of the year to say "I love you." Aside from the obvious traditional method of giving gifts, we suggest some other activities to make your next Christmas one that is filled with love for those special people in your life.

Here are some ways to say "I love you" to those in your family or to others who are especially close.

- Promise to do most of the Christmas shopping this coming year.
- Volunteer to wrap all the gifts.
- Take them out to look at the city's Christmas lights.
- Cook the Christmas dinner.
- Spend a little more money on them this year, if you can afford it.
- Invite close friends over to sing Christmas carols.

- Spend a night at home roasting chestnuts or popping corn in the fireplace.
- Build a snowman together.
- If you're far from home, surprise loved ones with a visit.

Sharing with Some Other Family:

This Christmas the love within your own family can be multiplied many times over if you make it a special year for some less fortunate family. Call your local social services office or a church to find out the name of a family needing help. Here are some ideas of what you can do for them:

- Find out the ages of the children and buy each an appropriate gift.
- Surprise them one evening with a Christmas tree and ornaments.
- Invite them to join your family for Christmas dinner.
- The most appropriate actions might best be done anonymously, like donating a turkey for the family's Christmas dinner.

51 ♥ Just Say It!

*You have seen so many new ways
Yet you know that you're never
   through
So practice a lot throughout all your
   days
By saying the words, "I love you"*

The Idea: We can't state it much more simply than the title of this suggestion. Just say it! We've shown you some clever ways to spend time with the ones you love, to express your feelings for them, and to have a lot of fun in the process. Throughout every day, we all could use another affirmation that we are loved.

Here are some simple, everyday activities you can do to encourage and remind those around you that they are loved.

- Give simple, inexpensive gifts on unexpected days.
- Dance with your loved one in your living room.
- Tell the people you love you are grateful for their friendship.
- Send them a FAX that says "I love you."
- Pray with them.
- Say "I'm sorry," "I was wrong," or "Please forgive me" when it needs to be said.
- Send a greeting card for no specific reason.
- Greet them with a smile and a hug every day.

- Write a special someone a love letter.
- Buy them a pet.
- Hold them when they cry.
- Stay home with your loved one an extra night in the week.
- Learn how to say "I love you" in sign language.
- Walk up, put your arms around someone you love, and say, "I love you."

52 ♥ Your Turn

Now that you've seen our fifty-one
Together we'll do fifty-two
Think of the ways that you have
had fun
In telling your friends "I love you"

The Idea: As you've been reading this book you may have thought of some ideas of your own. All along you may have been saying to yourself, "These guys didn't even include the idea that really worked for me. I remember the time I. . . ."

Racking Your Brain: Spend some time thinking about those activities you have done in the past that have really told those in your life how much you love them. Or, think of that friend of yours who always comes up with romantic ideas. What would he or she try?

List Your Own Ideas. Save them for a rainy day. Who knows, you may have enough to last a lifetime.

Send in Your Ideas. If you have thought of other simple ways to say "I love you," send them to:

Simple Ways to Say "I Love You"
c/o Carl Dreizler
P. O. Box 4788
Laguna Beach, CA 92652

Maybe your idea will be in print some day—which reminds us of another way to say "I love you." Share your ideas with others so they too will learn even more ways to say "I love you."

 # Afterword

What we've tried to do in this book is to create more ways to bring love to a sometimes loveless world. We hope you will use our ideas to tell all of the special people in your life how much they mean to you.

Mother Teresa has aptly said that people in America are dying (spiritually) from emotional hunger. We Americans have the resources to end this emotional famine. Three short words spoken sincerely have the power to satisfy our craving. Those three words are "I love you."